Why Does Earth Have Seasons?

by Marne Ventura

childsworld.com

Published by The Child's World®
1980 Lookout Drive • Mankato, MN 56003-1705
800-599-READ • www.childsworld.com

Acknowledgments
The Child's World®: Mary Swensen, Publishing Director
Red Line Editorial: Editorial direction and production
The Design Lab: Design

Photographs ©: Shutterstock Images, cover, 1, 7, 15, 17; Serge
Vero/Shutterstock Images, 5; NASA, 8; Red Line Editorial,
11, 13; Matyas Rehak/Shutterstock Images, 18; Anton Ivanov/
Shutterstock Images, 19; Betty Shelton/Shutterstock Images, 21

ISBN 9781503807983
LCCN 2015958218

Printed in the United States of America
Mankato, MN
June, 2016
PA02299

ABOUT THE AUTHOR

Marne Ventura writes fiction and nonfiction books for children. A former elementary school teacher, she holds a master's degree in education. Marne lives with her husband on the central coast of California.

TABLE of CONTENTS

CHAPTER 1

How Does Earth Move?

Most life on Earth needs the sun. Its rays warm the air and water. Plants use sunlight to grow. People eat plants for food. Without energy from the sun, the surface of the Earth would freeze. There would be no life on it.

Earth has four seasons. The seasons are spring, summer, fall, and winter. In most places, the weather changes with the seasons. Each season lasts for three months. New plants grow in spring. Snow melts. The air warms in summer. Days are longer. The air cools in fall.

In spring, snow melts. Some flowers bloom
before all the snow has melted.

Plant growth slows. Some places have snow in winter. The weather is cold. Why does Earth have seasons?

Earth is always moving. So why do we not feel it? It is because we move with it! The speed is constant. It is like riding in an airplane. Airplanes fly fast in the air. They travel at 550 miles per hour (885 kmh). But people inside the plane do not feel it. They are moving with the airplane.

Rotation is one way Earth moves. It spins on its axis. An axis is like an imaginary rod. It runs through the center of Earth. It takes one day for Earth

A rod goes through the center of this globe. It allows the globe to spin just as Earth does.

to spin around. One day is 24 hours. Earth also circles around the sun. One trip around the sun takes a year.

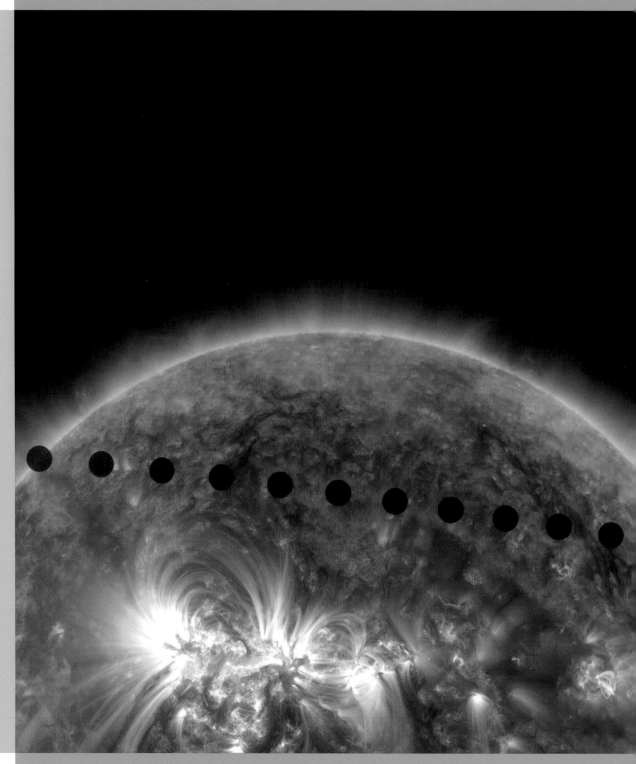

Venus is another planet that circles the sun. The dark circles show its path around the sun.

But Earth's path is not a perfect circle. It is like an oval. This means that sometimes Earth is closer to the sun than other times. Some people think that is why the seasons change. Do you? The truth is the change in distance is too small to cause seasons. In fact, Earth is closer to the sun when some parts have winter. Earth is farther from the sun when some parts have summer.

So what does cause the seasons? The answer has to do with Earth's axis and its angle.

CHAPTER 2

How Does the Movement of Earth Cause Seasons?

Imagine a line around the middle of Earth. It separates the top and bottom in half. The top half is the northern **hemisphere**. The bottom half is the southern hemisphere. The line is the **equator**.

Remember that Earth spins on its axis. The ends of the axis are called poles. The North Pole is on the top half. The South Pole is on the bottom half. But the planet is not straight up and down. Earth is tipped on its axis. The North Pole points toward the North Star. Earth is tipped at an angle of 23.5 degrees. The angle stays the same even as Earth moves. The poles always point the same way.

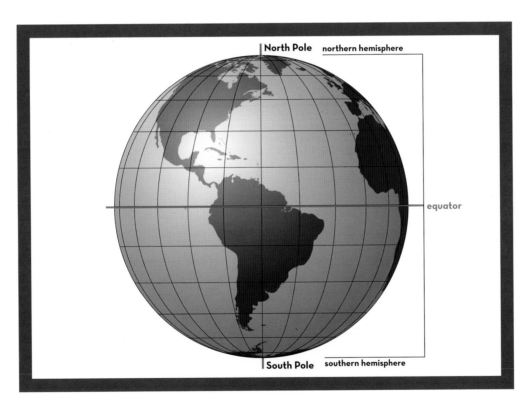

The equator divides Earth in half.

The top half is tipped toward the sun for six months. The bottom half is tipped away from the sun. Then the opposite happens. The bottom half is tipped toward the sun for the next six months. The top half is tipped away from the sun.

The half that is pointed toward the sun gets stronger light and heat. The weather is warmer. The half that is pointed away from the sun gets weaker light and heat. The weather is cooler. The angle of the sun's rays is different. This is what causes the seasons!

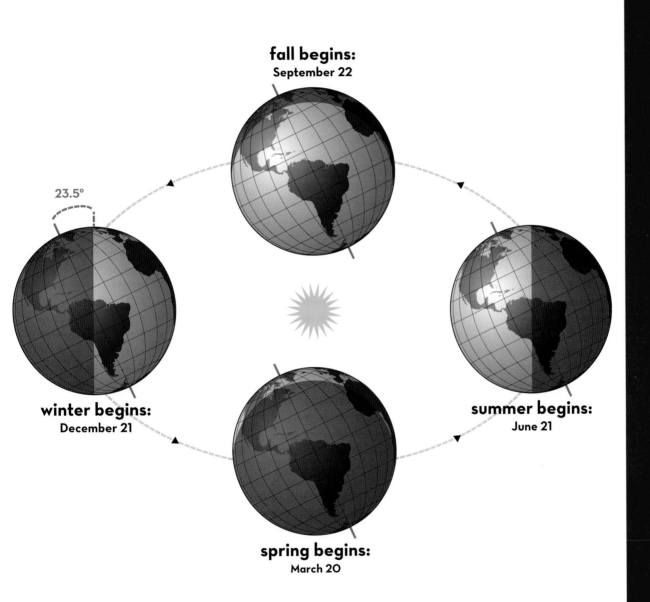

fall begins:
September 22

23.5°

winter begins:
December 21

summer begins:
June 21

spring begins:
March 20

This is how the seasons change in the northern hemisphere.

CHAPTER 3

How Do Seasons Change in Different Parts of Earth?

The seasons change near the 21st days of March, June, September, and December. Winter starts in December in the northern hemisphere. Spring starts in March. Summer starts in June. Fall starts in September. In the southern hemisphere, it is the opposite. Summer starts in December. Fall starts in March. Winter starts in June. Spring starts in September. In January, children in the north play in the snow. Children in the south play at the beach.

Many people in New Zealand celebrate New Year's Day by going to the beach. They enjoy the summer weather.

The length of a day changes with the seasons, too. The length of a day is the time between sunrise and sunset. The longest day of the year is the first day of summer. This is the summer **solstice**. The shortest day of the year is the first day of winter. This is the winter solstice. On the first day of spring and fall, the **equinox** occurs. Those days are special. The length of a day is the same as the length of a night.

Temperatures do not change much at the equator. The sun's rays land at about the same angle all year long. Heat and light from the sun are right overhead.

After the first day of fall, there are fewer daylight hours than nighttime hours.

Weather stays warm. The length of a day stays about the same, too.

The farther away a place is from the equator, the cooler it is. This is because

Some places near the equator have only two seasons: rainy and dry.

There is ice near the South Pole all year, even in summer.

the sun's rays are not right overhead.
The North and South Poles are never
tipped straight into the sunlight. Weather
at the poles is cold all year. In midwinter,
a pole is tipped away from the sun.

It gets no daylight at all. There is darkness for 24 hours. In midsummer, a pole is tipped toward the sun. There is daylight for 24 hours. There is no night.

Earth moves around the sun. But Earth also spins on its axis. The axis is tilted. This is what causes the seasons. The northern hemisphere tilts away from the sun. This causes winter in the north. The southern hemisphere tilts toward the sun. This causes summer in the south. Six months later, things change. The northern hemisphere tilts toward the sun. It is summer. The southern hemisphere tilts away from the sun. It is winter.

Animals react to the changing seasons, too.
Baby deer are born in early summer.

21

The Angle of Sunlight

See how the sun's energy reaches Earth differently in summer and winter.

What You Need
flashlight
2 pieces of paper
pencil

What to Do
1. Turn on a small flashlight and hold it about one foot (30 cm) above a piece of paper. Trace the edges of the light with a pencil.
2. Use a new piece of paper. Shine the light on it from the same distance away, but at an angle. Trace the lighted area with a pencil.
3. How are the drawings different? When the light is directly overhead (summer), it is gathered in a smaller area. The weather is warmer. When the same amount of light comes in at an angle (winter), it is spread out over a bigger area. The weather is cooler.

Glossary

equator (i-KWAY-tur) The equator is an imaginary line around Earth, midway between the North and South Poles. Weather at the equator gets direct sunlight year round.

equinox (EE-kwuh-nahks) The equinox is a day on Earth when the length of darkness and daylight are equal. The spring equinox in the north is usually March 20 and the fall equinox is usually September 22.

hemisphere (HEM-i-sfeer) A hemisphere is one half of Earth. Earth is divided into the northern and southern hemispheres.

rotation (roh-TAY-shun) Rotation is the movement of spinning on an axis. Earth completes one rotation on its axis each day.

solstice (SOHL-stis) A solstice is a day during the year that has either the longest length of daylight (summer) or the shortest length of daylight (winter). The summer solstice in the north is usually June 21, and the winter solstice is usually December 21.

To Learn More

In the Library

Auteri, Linda. *Winter, Spring, Summer, Fall!* Franklin Lakes, NJ: Chrantin Publishing, 2012.

Esbaum, Jill. *Winter Wonderland.* Washington, DC: National Geographic Kids, 2010.

Herrington, Lisa M. *How Do You Know It's Summer?* New York: Scholastic, 2013.

On the Web

Visit our Web site for links about Earth's seasons: **childsworld.com/links**

Note to Parents, Teachers, and Librarians: We routinely verify our Web links to make sure they are safe and active sites. So encourage your readers to check them out!

Index